BEARPORT BIOGRAPHIES

OLIVIA RODRIGO

ACTOR AND SINGER

by Rachel Rose

Minneapolis, Minnesota

Credits

Cover and Title page, © Jon Kopaloff/Getty Images; 4, © David Becker/Stringer/Getty Images; 5, © Rich Fury/Staff/Getty Images; 6, © tyasindayanti/Shutterstock; 7, © Ron and Patty Thomas/iStock; 9, © David Livingston/Contributor/Getty Images; 10, © A.D.Portrat/Shutterstock; 11, © Walt Disney Television/flickr.com; 12, © Frazer Harrison/Staff/Getty Images; 13, © Jenny Anderson/Stringer/Getty Images; 14, © Kevin Mazur/Contributor/Getty Images; 15, © Kevin Mazur/MTV VMAs 2021/Contributor/Getty Images; 16, © MICHAEL TRAN/Contributor/Getty Images; 17, © Rich Polk/Stringer/Getty Images; 18, © RandomUserGuy1738/Wikimedia; 19, © The Washington Post/Contributor/Getty Images; 20, © Joseph Okpako/Contributor/Getty Images; 21, © Kathy Hutchins/Shutterstock

Bearport Publishing Company Product Development Team

President: Jen Jenson; Director of Product Development: Spencer Brinker; Senior Editor: Allison Juda; Editor: Charly Haley; Associate Editor: Naomi Reich; Senior Designer: Colin O'Dea; Associate Designer: Elena Klinkner; Associate Designer: Kayla Eggert; Product Development Assistant: Anita Stasson

Library of Congress Cataloging-in-Publication Data

Names: Rose, Rachel, 1968- author.
Title: Olivia Rodrigo : actor and singer / by Rachel Rose.
Description: Minneapolis, Minnesota : Bearport Publishing Company, 2023. | Series: Bearport biographies | Includes bibliographical references and index.
Identifiers: LCCN 2022038960 (print) | LCCN 2022038961 (ebook) | ISBN 9798885094047 (library binding) | ISBN 9798885095266 (paperback) | ISBN 9798885096416 (ebook)
Subjects: LCSH: Rodrigo, Olivia--Juvenile literature. | Singers--United States--Biography--Juvenile literature. | Actors--United States--Biography--Juvenile literature. | LCGFT: Biographies.
Classification: LCC ML3930.R634 R66 2023 (print) | LCC ML3930.R634 (ebook) | DDC 782.42164092 [B]--dc23
LC record available at https://lccn.loc.gov/2022038960
LC ebook record available at https://lccn.loc.gov/2022038961

Copyright © 2023 Bearport Publishing Company. All rights reserved. No part of this publication may be reproduced in whole or in part, stored in any retrieval system, or transmitted in any form or by any means, electronic, mechanical, photocopying, recording, or otherwise, without written permission from the publisher.

For more information, write to Bearport Publishing, 5357 Penn Avenue South, Minneapolis, MN 55419.

Contents

Three-Time Winner **4**

Childhood Dreams **6**

Acting the Part **10**

Pop Star **14**

Speaking Up **18**

What's Next? **20**

Timeline 22

Glossary 23

Index 24

Read More 24

Learn More Online 24

About the Author 24

Three-Time Winner

Olivia Rodrigo cried tears of joy as she looked out at the **audience**. The young singer had just won the 2022 Grammy **Award** for Best Pop Vocal Album. It was her third award of the night. Olivia had dreamed of this moment since she was a little kid, and she worked hard to make her dream come true!

Later in the night, Olivia accidentally dropped one of her awards. She broke it.

Childhood Dreams

Olivia was born on February 20, 2003. Growing up in Temecula, California, she was a busy kid! Olivia started taking singing lessons and acting classes by the time she was six. By age seven, she was singing in talent **contests**. It wasn't long before she started going to acting **auditions**.

Part of Olivia's family is from the Philippines in Asia. Growing up, she loved to cook Filipino food with her parents.

Oliva's favorite Filipino food to make is called lumpia (LOOM-pee-uh).

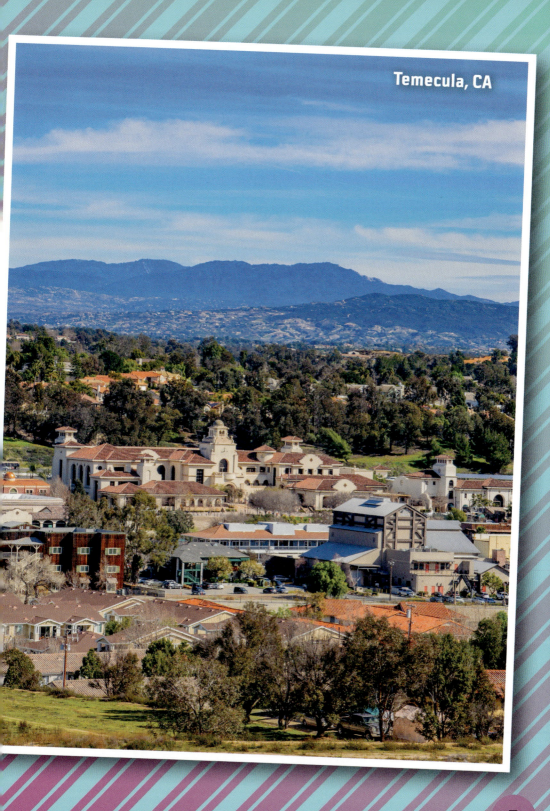
Temecula, CA

At first, Olivia wasn't offered any acting parts. But she didn't let it stop her. She kept trying to get any role she could find. Then, she had her first big break. When Olivia was 10, she was picked to star in the movie *An American Girl: Grace Stirs Up Success*.

Olivia would often travel almost 90 miles (145 km) for auditions.

Acting the Part

Olivia's acting **career** took off. She got the part of Paige on the TV show *Bizaardvark*. For this role, Olivia had some homework to do. She needed to learn to play the guitar! Soon, she started writing her own songs on the instrument. She was happy to bring music into her acting role.

Although she became famous for acting first, Olivia thinks of herself as a singer who became an actor.

Olivia attended the 2016 Radio Disney Music Awards.

In 2019, Olivia got a starring role on the TV show *High School Musical: The Musical: The Series*. Instantly, she felt connected with her character Nini, whose **passions** were music and theater. Not long after getting the role, Olivia wrote a song for her character to sing. It was a huge success. A few **record companies** began to take notice.

Olivia (second from right) with her costars at the premiere for HSMTMTS.

Olivia helped write a couple of songs for the show. They became fan favorites!

Olivia and Joshua Bassett sing songs from *HSMTMTS* during a live event.

Pop Star

While continuing to act, Olivia began making her own music. In 2021, she came out with her first song, called "Drivers License." Olivia wrote a song she wanted to sing and not what she thought might do well on pop music charts. But the singer quickly found her song racing to the top.

"Drivers License" was the first song of 2021 to be played over 1 billion times!

"Drivers License" won the 2021 Song of the Year Award at the MTV Video Music Awards.

15

Olivia learned a lot while writing and recording her music. The experience not only taught her about music but also a lot about herself. She hoped people would enjoy the honesty in her songs. Olivia was **excited** to share her first full album, titled *Sour*. The new songs were a hit!

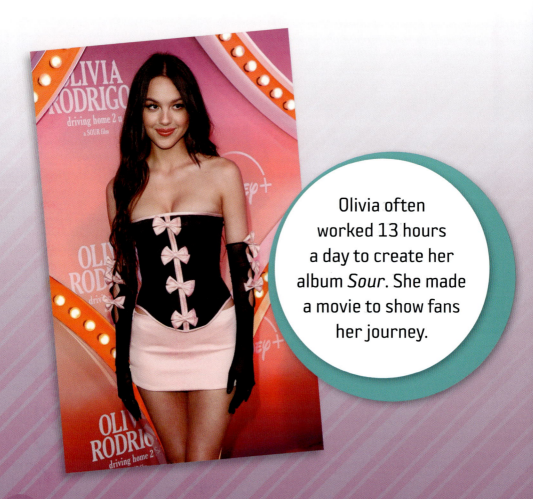

Olivia often worked 13 hours a day to create her album *Sour*. She made a movie to show fans her journey.

Olivia won an award for the movie she made about her album.

Speaking Up

Music is just one way Olivia shares her life with fans. She also speaks up about what she believes in. In 2021, Olivia was invited to the White House by President Joe Biden. From the famous building, Olivia spoke to her fans and other young people across America. She **encouraged** everyone to stay safe from COVID-19 by getting **vaccinated**.

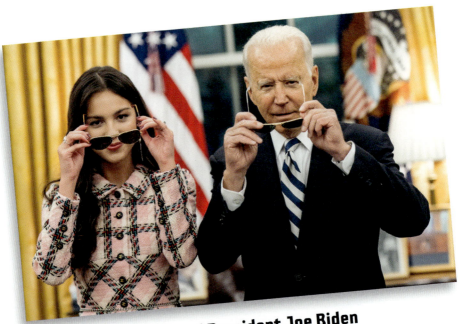

Olivia and President Joe Biden strike a fun pose in the Oval Office.

Olivia shared a video of her speaking at the White House with her 28 million fans on social media.

Olivia does what she can to help the **environment**, too. She will often buy used clothes instead of new ones.

What's Next?

Olivia has done a lot to make her dreams come true. She became an actor and continued to make music a part of her life. Then, she followed her passion to become a pop star. There is still so much ahead for Olivia—and she is excited for everything the future has to offer!

Someday, Olivia wants to write songs for other singers.

Timeline

Here are some key dates in Olivia Rodrigo's Life.

2003 Born on February 20

2013 Lands starring role in her first movie

2016 Gets the lead role in *Bizaardvark*

2019 Stars in *High School Musical: The Musical: The Series*

2021 Comes out with *Sour*

2021 Speaks at the White House

2022 Wins three Grammys

22

Glossary

audience a group of people listening to or looking at something

auditions things actors do to see if they are right for a part

award a prize for being the best at something

career a lifelong job

contests competitions where two or more people try to be the best at something, usually for a prize

encouraged supported another person

environment the natural world

excited to be very happy about something

passions the things a person cares about very deeply

record companies the businesses that make and sell music

vaccinated given medicine that helps protect against disease

Index

An American Girl: Grace Stirs Up Success 8
auditions 6, 8
award 4, 11, 15, 17
Biden, Joe 18
Bizaardvark 10, 22
career 10
COVID-19 18
"Drivers License" 14-15
High School Musical: The Musical: The Series 12-13, 22
Philippines 6
Sour 16, 22
Temecula, CA 6-7
The White House 18-19, 22

Read More

Abdo, Kenny. *Pop Music History (Musical Notes)*. Minneapolis: Abdo Zoom, 2020.

Schwartz, Heather E. *Olivia Rodrigo: Hit Singer-Songwriter (In the Spotlight)*. Minneapolis: Lerner Publications, 2022.

Learn More Online

1. Go to **www.factsurfer.com** or scan the QR code below.
2. Enter "**Olivia Rodrigo**" into the search box.
3. Click on the cover of this book to see a list of websites.

About the Author

Rachel Rose is a writer who lives in San Francisco. Her favorite books to write are about people who lead inspiring lives.

24